Ritual for Dolls

a play

George MacEwan Green

ISBN 978 0 573 12231 6

CHARACTERS

This play was first presented at the 1969 National Union of Students' Drama Festival by the Leicester University Theatre with the following cast:

Arabella, an old-fashioned Alice-in-Wonderland type of doll
Margot Leicester

Bravo, a red-coated soldier doll   Leslie Perrin
Golly, a golliwog   Robert Moger
Jo-Jo, a clockwork monkey with a toy drum   Steve Silver

RITUAL FOR DOLLS

Part of an attic. C.S. is a large, gaily painted box, its lid open   The box
contains the characters of the play   To one side of the stage there is also a
wooden cube, like an enlarged lettered play-brick. There is a rathole in the
skirting board. When the curtain rises a clock is heard striking twelve.
After the twelfth stroke JO-JO rises up in the box, very slowly and painfully,
and stiffly gives a rat-tat-tat upon his drum. GOLLY rises wearily, looks
around and smiles.

GOLLY   What's this then, man, another midnight? Lord Almighty,
                         they seem to come round faster 'n' faster every day – or,
                         maybe, I mean every night.   (He climbs out of box
                         and struts about as if loosening his joints.)   I tell you,
                         Jo-Jo man, there was a time when midnights were
                         decently spaced out every twenty-four hours, just the way
                         the good God intended.   (He goes to box, bangs upon
                         it and then flops over to peer down inside of it.)
                         Rise and shine, you two. Come on now, Miss Arabella,
                         show a leg. Wakey-wakey, Lieutenant Bravo. It done
                         strike twelve of the clock.   (Begins to move across
                         stage.)   Jo-Jo here been up and drumming long since,
                         God and the world's asleep and   (Peers down into
                         rat-hole.)   them mean ole rats is having them a ball
                         behind the skirting boards.   (He sits down upon the
                         cube, stretching his legs luxuriously.)

(JO-JO beats his drum again persistently   BRAVO springs up in the box angrily)

BRAVO   Do you mind? I say, do you mind?

(JO-JO's drumming begins to tail off.)

You know, Golly, we could do very well without your nightly salutation to the enchanted hour. And as for you, Jo-Jo, would you please put a bloody sock in it

(JO-JO moodily stops drumming.)

That damn drum of yours has been the bane of my life for as long as I can remember.

(JO-JO drums once and BRAVO gets out of box and does knees-bend, while GOLLY does touchtoes on the cube. ARABELLA rises laboriously.)

ARABELLA   What's happening? Eh? Huh? Oh God, can't you fellows let a lady get her beauty sleep in peace? Mamma, Mamma, Mamma.   (To JO-JO.)   See what you've done? Mamma, Mamma, Mamma, Mamma   I've got a fit of the Mammas now

(BRAVO claps her heartily upon the back.)

(Squealing.)   M-m- aaa - mm - aaa

BRAVO   Better, old girl?

ARABELLA   Yes, but I'd rather you didn't do that. My guts are all to hell as it is, without you thumping more of my inwards off balance.

GOLLY   (jumping from cube and crossing to box)   Come on then, lady and gents, it's that old enchanted hour and we got to do our enchanting.

ARABELLA   (to GOLLY and mimicking)   And we got to do our enchanting.   (To BRAVO.)   If there's one thing I detest it's an eager-beaver wog.

BRAVO   Yes, Golly, old man, do try to moderate your enthusiasm. Gentlemen avoid excess in all things, don't you know? (He marches across stage and sits stiffly on the cube.)

GOLLY   (following BRAVO and jabbing him)   Enthusiastic?

Me? Let me tell you, soldier boy, I'm enthusiastic about
nothing, less 'n' it be about folding up my sawdust and
getting the ole head down inside of this here box.
(Returns to box and helps ARABELLA out of it.)   No,
sir, I'm not the enthusiastic one, but the way I see it, we
is nature-bound to do our bit of enchanting come every
midnight and to my mind – simple though it be –

ARABELLA   You said it, nigger boy   (Dusting herself down.)

GOLLY   – simple though it be – I reckon we might as well get it
            over with just as fast as we can   No sense railing against
            what's got to be.

            (ARABELLA yawns.)

BRAVO   What cannot be changed must be endured? I suppose you
            do have a point, comrade, but do let's have the grit
            without the grins.

ARABELLA   (pointing to JO-JO struggling in box)   We shall never
            start until that damn fool monkey gets his leg over the edge

            (They all stare at JO-JO who is unsuccessfully trying to
            raise a leg.

GOLLY   Man, that's a sad sight. Why, I can recall the time when
            that Jo-Jo could leap outa that box like a roe-deer
            clearing a hedge.   (He assists JO-JO out of the box.)

BRAVO   Age is an awesome thing. It is the one mirror hateful to
            the vanity of Youth. Come on, old campaigner, let me
            give you a hand.

            (BRAVO goes over to help JO-JO who is now out of the
            box.)

ARABELLA   Before I reach that stage I pray to God I burst a gut, or my
            head falls off.

BRAVO   Don't be morbid, dear.   (Stamps his foot in military
            fashion)   Now, let's all get fell in

            (JO-JO, GOLLY and ARABELLA line up in front of the
            box, leaving a space between GOLLY and ARABELLA later
            to be filled by BRAVO. BRAVO walks along the line
            inspecting each, making a point of adjusting JO-JO's arms
            and brushing dust from GOLLY's lapels. When he reaches

          the end of the line and while his back is still turned upon the others, JO-JO gives a sudden tap upon the drum This makes BRAVO start and he turns sharply to stare accusingly)

BRAVO   Now, who'll begin?

ARABELLA   Oh, let lay-preacher wog start as usual. He has such a natural bent for it

BRAVO   So be it   (He takes his place in the line.)   On your mark, Golly

          (JO-JO gives three beats upon drum and GOLLY steps forward.)

GOLLY   In the beginning was the children, and lo, the toys was created for their satisfaction The children strived after fulfilment and the toys was their handservants in their striving. Thus was it ordained and thus it was and thus will it be hereafter until the end of children and the end of toys.

          (Drum sounds and GOLLY steps back into line. BRAVO steps out.)

BRAVO   In the beginning were the games and the imaginings and the dreams, and blessed were the children for they sought joy, and blessed were the toys for they were the way and the life.

          (Drum sounds and BRAVO steps back into line ARABELLA steps out)

ARABELLA   In the beginning there was innocence and there was purity and there was nothing which was unclean of mind or spirit

          (Drum sounds and ARABELLA steps back into line.)

GOLLY   There was laughter --

BRAVO   And learning --

ARABELLA   And loving.

GOLLY   It was all according to what was divinely intended --

BRAVO   And it was good --

ARABELLA   And it was a part of the whole

GOLLY   Somewhere in the house there was Papa,

             (BRAVO moves out of line and crosses to the cube where
             he stretches out his hands, as if warming them at a fire.)

             smelling of clean linen and starched collars and tobacco
             and, occasionally, the heady perfume of his mistress. He
             spoke with the tongue of authority and the house listened
             When he spoke in a voice of anger the house trembled -

ARABELLA   Deliciously

             (BRAVO moves back in front of others.)

BRAVO   (gruffly and boomingly)   Money does not grow on
             trees - a wife's duty and a woman's place - mind your
             manners, Miss - have a care, boy, do you hear? I shall
             be obeyed - I shall be obeyed   (He returns to his
             place in the line)

GOLLY   And somewhere in the house was Mamma, moving about in
             the rustle of stiffened taffeta and the tinkling of teacups.
             When she whispered the house strained to listen -

ARABELLA   Such gloriously vindictive whispers, tearing whole
             reputations to shreds with such sweet gentility

GOLLY   And when she shrieked

             (ARABELLA steps out of line.)

             the house prickled all over and stopped up its ears.

             (ARABELLA rounds upon the line)

ARABELLA   (in high-pitched, peevish voice)   Don't think I don't
             know what you've been up to and who you've been with -
             you reek of that wicked woman - you crucify me with your
             infidelity - children be silent - my migraine - my nerves -
             my heart.   (She returns to place in the line)

GOLLY   And there was Holdsome, the butler -

             (BRAVO steps forward.)

BRAVO   Dinner is served, madam   (He returns to line.)

GOLLY   And Bagworth, the cook -

             (ARABELLA steps forward.)

ARABELLA   And what can they expect if they'll only buy bleeding
                scrag-end. I'm a cook, not a ruddy miracle worker.
                (She sniffs, tosses head and returns to line.)

GOLLY   And Annie Fluck, the housemaid -

                (BRAVO pinches ARABELLA and she, giggling, jumps out
                sideways.)

ARABELLA   Lawks, sir, whatever would the Missis say if she saw us?
                (She steps back into line.)

GOLLY   And there was the children, the blessed dear and lovely
                children.

BRAVO   There was Master Percival - a brave, stout-hearted,
                tender-souled little chap.

ARABELLA   And there was his sister - his dear, dear sister Alice - a
                sweet, twinkling-eyed, warm-hearted little lady.

GOLLY   They was good and kind and loving to their toys.
                (He walks over to cube and sits down.)   Great God in
                the morning, I can still feel the softness of Miss Alice's
                cheek against my own, as she hugged me and hugged me
                fit to burst my seams.

BRAVO   That's true enough. That's undeniable   They had a
                wealth of affection for us.   (To ARABELLA.)   I can
                remember that splendid boy, Master Percival, pouring his
                dreams into every atom of my being and often Miss Alice
                would tell me how handsome and gallant I was.

                (ARABELLA steps forward.)

ARABELLA   There was one time when Master Percival sneaked in here,
                lifted me out of the doll's house -   (To BRAVO.)
                in those days I actually slept in a doll's house.   (To
                GOLLY.)   I didn't dorm in a rotten, old box -
                anyway, Master Percival lifted me out and carried me back
                to his own little bed. There, under the blankets and
                nestled in his arms, he whispered into my ear everything
                that was in his heart

                (GOLLY gets up and moves towards ARABELLA.)

GOLLY   You never done told us that before, Miss Arabella.

ARABELLA   Well, I'm telling you now, so there

BRAVO   Into his bed? You?

ARABELLA   I just said so, didn't I?

BRAVO   Yes, I know - but,   mean to say, old girl - well, how
                 old was he?

ARABELLA   How should I know? He was a child - ten or eleven or
                 twelve, I suppose   Why are you looking at me like that?
                 (To BRAVO.)   He was a child and I was a doll.
                 (To GOLLY.)   I was a toy and he loved toys.

GOLLY   Yes, they done both loved toys, Master Percival and Miss
                 Alice.

                 (JO-JO beats impatiently upon his drum. GOLLY puts an
                 arm around JO-JO.)

GOLLY   )
BRAVO   )   Yes, they even loved old Jo-Jo.
ARABELLA   )

GOLLY   (stepping forward)   Such loving children.

BRAVO   (stepping forward)   And they loved each other.

ARABELLA   (stepping forward)   How they loved each other

GOLLY   They loved -

BRAVO   As brother and sister -

ARABELLA   Rarely love.

                 (JO-JO beats drum furiously   The drumming dies.)

GOLLY   (turning to others)   Then they was all growed up and
                 they put their toys aside.

BRAVO   (turning to others)   But they did not forget us. Neither
                 did we forget them.

ARABELLA   (turning to others)   Forget them? How could we? The
                 only life we had was what they had breathed into us.

                 (They all snap back into line.)

                 We had grown apace, we toys and the children, because
                 we had grown as one. That relationship might be set aside,
                 but it could not be forgotten

GOLLY   Master Percival, he crossed the ocean. He went to that
               dark, hot place from whence sprang the very essence of my
               being. He went to Africa

BRAVO   He was a true son of Empire   Right through the core of his
               personality ran the thin, hard, unbreakable band of steel
               labelled 'Duty'   He knew his place was in Africa.

               (BRAVO and ARABELLA embrace   BRAVO marches over to
               cube, whilst JO-JO drums. GOLLY and JO-JO move
               U S. where JO-JO squats by the rat-hole and drums
               quietly and in African style with his finger-tips.
               ARABELLA waves. BRAVO places a foot upon the cube
               and, as if he had a writing pad upon his knee, pretends to
               write)

               Dearest Sister Alice, I am arrived at Swamali where I take
               up my duties as District Officer   It is searingly hot and
               oppressive   Life here is dark and primitive and one feels
               that one has put ones shoulder to a huge, massive wheel
               which will forever refuse to turn -

ARABELLA   (pretending to read letter)   - or if it should turn will
               only roll backwards and utterly crush the one who pushes.
               I can only endure because I know I must and because I
               have such a host of blessed memories from which to draw
               strength. Those memories are of you, dearest Sister Alice,
               and of the happy, happy days we shared. Bereft of such
               memories I should become one of the living dead   I send
               my kisses of undying gratitude   (She closes letter.)

GOLLY   Papa died.

               (JO-JO beats drum solemnly.)

               Then Mamma died.

               (Again drum.)

BRAVO   Dearest Sister Alice, I would come to you with all my
               heart, for at this moment we should be together, but I am
               tied to this place by the fetters of responsibility   They are
               such children, my golliwogs, and depend upon me so.
               Since I cannot come to you, may I urge you to think about
               joining me here. Be not mistaken -

ARABELLA   Be not mistaken, it is a hard place for a woman. It is all

but comfortless. It is harsh and unrelenting. And yet, my
dearest Alice, if you would come –

BRAVO   – for me at least it would be transformed into the most
precious of places.

ARABELLA   I come, my dear, I come

GOLLY   And so Miss Alice locked up this big, old house and off she
went across the mighty seas to Golliwog land and to her
brother, Percival.

(JO-JO beats drum   ARABELLA moves over to cube where
she and BRAVO embrace. ARABELLA sits down on cube.)

ARABELLA   (as if writing)   Dear Journal, it is so gratifying to be
with dear Percival   Swamali is not nearly so terrible as he
led me to believe   In truth, it is extremely hot and such
few facilities as exist are of the crudest kind.   (She
rises and moves C.S.)   On the other hand, the
atmosphere is electric with a sense of raw, savage life and
this I find stimulating. The people are still untamed –

(GOLLY approaches ARABELLA and rhythmically encircles
her while JO-JO beats his drum. Then GOLLY kneels
down.)

– still untamed, but some of them possess the most noble
bearing. They are such sensual and innocent children

(BRAVO stares at ARABELLA and GOLLY sternly   Then he
faces audience, comes to attention and salutes.)

BRAVO   I have the honour to submit to your Excellency my report
upon the current position in this district   The majority of
the indigenous population under my jurisdiction are
peaceful and law-abiding and eager to avail themselves of
the benefits of our Christian civilisation   I must, however,
tell your Excellency that there are a few who are so firmly
shackled to the sinister and superstition-ridden customs of
their own culture that they are beyond redemption
Although scant in number they could be powerfully
instrumental in retarding the advancement of the majority
In other words, they could well prove dangerous and may
yet have to be dealt with in no half-measure manner.

(JO-JO beats rapidly   BRAVO salutes and then moves to

join ARABELLA C.S. He takes her arm and they walk
towards the cube)

BRAVO   Soon my spell of duty will be finished here, dearest Alice.
Then we shall return home. It will be as it used to be   I
shall take you away from this hateful place, this accursed,
filthy hole

ARABELLA   But, Percival, I don't mind it. On the contrary, I rather
enjoy it   One knows one is alive. Listen

(JO-JO beats drum louder)

That is the sound of their heart beat. They have a strong,
vibrant heart beat, do they not?   (She wriggles from
BRAVO's grasp and moves towards C.S.)   I have grown
to love the people so.

BRAVO   Love?

ARABELLA   Well, admire them.

BRAVO   But they have no intelligence, no wit, no staying power
even.   (He moves over to ARABELLA.)

ARABELLA   Oh, staying power they have, Percival   Like the trees of
their jungles they are deeply rooted. They know the
earth.

BRAVO   My dear, they can only scratch at the earth   They are the
most inept farmers in the world.

ARABELLA   They know the earth for what it really is - the untamable
provider   They know the earth as a man knows a woman,
as one soul knows another soul.

BRAVO   Such talk is unhealthy, Alice   I beg you not to speak so.
It grieves me and makes me feel peevish.   (He turns
away sharply from ARABELLA and moves to cube.)

ARABELLA   (watching him go)   Then, of course, I shall be silent
(Turns to look down at GOLLY and speaks quietly)
But I cannot promise not to think such things. When I look
upon them, when a word passes between us, when my hand
touches one of theirs I shall be thinking such things.

GOLLY   And do you suppose, Miss Alice, that I shall not be
thinking also? Do you know what I shall be thinking?

ARABELLA   (stepping back, surprised)   No, nor do I want to know I must not be told. You must only listen to what I say. (She kneels down by GOLLY.)   Let me see, what must I tell you? God made heaven and earth and all that in them is.

GOLLY   That was a mighty task.

ARABELLA   Yes, it took him all of six working days. What else? Ah yes, God sent his only begotten son.

GOLLY   He begot a son?

ARABELLA   Born of the Virgin Mary.

GOLLY   He took her into the bush and laid her and put a baba into her belly?

ARABELLA   Don't be uncouth. But, well, it was something like that. Not exactly, mind you, but a little like that   The child was Jesus and we crucified him

GOLLY   I didn't, Miss Alice

ARABELLA   Yes, you did, although you did not know about it   He said: 'Forgive them, for they know not what they do What do you think? No, don't tell me.   (She gets up and moves to C.S.)   Rather, I'll tell you about the great white queen across the seas, Her Brittanic Majesty Queen Victoria.

                (GOLLY gets up and goes round ARABELLA.)

GOLLY   The jolly, plump lady who has castors instead of feet?

ARABELLA   That's silly. She has feet

GOLLY   I know

ARABELLA   And she is not to be laughed at   Besides being good and kind and being the grandmother of Europe, she is also very powerful and at the raising of her little finger could, if she so pleased, demolish all the tribes of Africa   What do you think? No, do not tell me. Yes, do.

GOLLY   I think –

BRAVO   I have the honour to report to your Excellency that I may be forced to take strong and decisive action against such

as are plotting to thwart the natural course of our
civilising influence

GOLLY   I think, here is a woman frail and white and delicate   I
think, here is a woman who is weak of body   I think,
here am I, strong of limb and muscle   I think, here is a
woman who knows many things, carrying a great weight of
knowledge in her brain and here am I, ignorant and
untutored. I think, given these circumstances, we two
should cleave one to the other, supporting our weaknesses
one upon the other, letting our strengths flow betwixt body
and body

ARABELLA   (turning away from GOLLY)   Oh no, it cannot be. It
would be wrong. It makes sense and it would be entirely
wrong.

BRAVO   I have the honour to report to your Excellency that the
situation is far from satisfactory, and, indeed, that it
worsens daily   I feel I am being constantly spied upon
and, also, I feel that I, in turn, must constantly be spying.
I have the honour to tell your Excellency that I am afraid.
I love her, you see   I cannot believe that she would ever
give herself to one of them, but I have these fevered
nightmares in which she does just that.

GOLLY   It makes sense and it would be wrong. That is, my dear
Miss Alice, it would be wrong if there was not one other
factor to be taken into consideration.

ARABELLA   Factor?   (She turns back to look at GOLLY.)
What factor?

GOLLY   Love   Behold, my heart says to me, here is the love of
your life   Here is the one whose value is greater than the
gold from the soil of your homeland and more precious
than the rubies plucked from the rocks of your beloved
Africa

BRAVO   And in other nightmares, your Excellency, I see myself
taking her with hungry savagery. I awake feeling unclean,
diseased of mind and with the desire of my nightmares still
throbbing in my thighs. I detest myself for harbouring
such dreams and, dreaming, spill my seed upon the sheets
of my fever-soaked bed.

ARABELLA   Love. I will not have you say that word again. I worship
                you, my god of ebony. I adore you, my wild, exciting,
                heathen prince   You must not speak to me of love, for it
                is unseemly. Take me.

                (JO-JO beats louder upon his drum.)

BRAVO   Your Excellency must know that there are some things a
                man – even a white man and a loyal servant of the Crown –
                cannot endure. Some things cannot be lived with. I trust
                her ladyship is enjoying good health   I am at the end of
                my tether   I must congratulate your Excellency upon the
                splendid achievements of your Excellency's polo team
                For God's sake, does no one care that I am going mad? I
                want her   I crave her   Does your Excellency hear?
                (Turns to others.)   I desire carnal knowledge of my
                sister Alice and I beg to report to your Excellency –

ARABELLA   Take me, black man   Love me, black man   Lay me upon
                the ground, black man   Consume me, Africa.
                (Holding GOLLY's hands, she kneels down in front of him
                Then she lies down)

                (GOLLY kneels down between ARABELLA's legs.)

BRAVO   And I beg to report to your Excellency that if I cannot
                have her   then by the living Christ I shall not stand by
                whilst some other man has his fill of her

GOLLY   Prepare, my white love, to take Africa to your breasts.
                (He starts to lie down)

                (JO-JO beats wildly   BRAVO lunges forward, as if
                dagger in hand, and smites GOLLY in the back. GOLLY
                falls forward across ARABELLA's body   The drumming
                stops.)

BRAVO   Can a dead man pleasure you, dearest Alice?   (He
                looks at his hands. He is shocked. He falls to his knees.)
                Gentle Jesus meek and mild – away in a manger – there
                is a green hill far away – all things bright and beautiful
                (Then with a great sob of agony)   Why?   (He
                buries his face in his hands and weeps.)

                (There is a pause   JO-JO drums. BRAVO, GOLLY and
                ARABELLA rise   They take up their stance in front of the

box. JO-JO stops drumming.)

GOLLY	Master Percival died of a fever in darkest Africa
BRAVO	There were rumours and rumours -
ARABELLA	And Africa was no longer a place for Miss Alice to be She came back to England.
BRAVO	She opened up this house again.
GOLLY	She is somewhere downstairs at this very moment. She is a wizened, ancient lady who wears a ragged old wig to hide the baldness of her head.
BRAVO	She has no teeth and exists from day to day upon slops.
ARABELLA	But at night she dreams of Africa.
	(A clock strikes one.)
GOLLY	(breaking the line) That's it over then, praise God. Let's hit the box. I'm fair tuckered out.
BRAVO	I must admit I, too, am a mite fatigued.
ARABELLA	(moving to box) I'm plain pooped.
BRAVO	(moving after ARABELLA) Allow me to assist you back into the box.
ARABELLA	I'll manage. You two see to that damn fool monkey. (She climbs into the box.)
	(BRAVO and GOLLY assist JO-JO into the box and then follow him. All four disappear from sight There is the sound of a yawn.)

CURTAIN

9 780573 122316